ALMA DEUTSCHER
FROM MY BOOK OF MELODIES

Edited by James Welland
Additionally edited by Daniel Rollison and Stephanie Woodworth
Music engraved by SEL Music Art Ltd
Cover photography by Phil Dera (www.phildera.net)

All the pieces from this volume are on Sony Classical
and available to listen to and/or purchase from all major streaming
services worldwide including Spotify, Apple Music, and Amazon.

ISBN 978-1-7051-3098-8

G. SCHIRMER Ltd.
part of **WiseMusic**Group

EXCLUSIVELY DISTRIBUTED BY

Copyright © 2020 by G. Schirmer Ltd.
International Copyright Secured All Rights Reserved

For all works contained herein:
Unauthorized copying, arranging, adapting, recording, internet posting, public performance,
or other distribution of the printed music in this publication is an infringement of copyright.
Infringers are liable under the law.

Visit Hal Leonard Online at
www.halleonard.com

Contact us:
Hal Leonard
7777 West Bluemound Road
Milwaukee, WI 53213
Email: info@halleonard.com

In Europe, contact:
Hal Leonard Europe Limited
42 Wigmore Street
Marylebone, London, W1U 2RN
Email: info@halleonardeurope.com

In Australia, contact:
Hal Leonard Australia Pty. Ltd.
4 Lentara Court
Cheltenham, Victoria, 3192 Australia
Email: info@halleonard.com.au

I started hearing melodies in my head when I was four years old. I pretended that they were songs from my imaginary country, which I called "Transylvanian". (I don't remember why I chose this name, but it had nothing to do with the real Transylvania.) When I was small, I couldn't write the music down, so I played my melodies on the piano and my parents would sometimes record them. But as soon as I learnt to write music, I started writing my melodies down in a notebook so that I wouldn't forget them. Actually, I don't just have one book of melodies, but a few notebooks. In some of them I wrote down whole pieces. In others I wrote only the first few bars of the melodies.

In 2019, I recorded a piano album for Sony Classical, where I chose one melody from each year of my life, from ages four to fourteen. And all the pieces from the album are included in this book. But maybe I should explain: the age when the melody first came to me is not always the same as when I composed the whole piece based on this melody. Very often, I would note down a melody, and then use it only later, sometimes years later, when I was composing a piece in which this melody would fit.

I hope you will enjoy playing these pieces.

Alma

CONTENTS

For Antonia (Variations on a melody in G major)

I improvised this melody on the piano when I was four. I couldn't write down notes then (or to be more accurate: I squiggled many notes, but no one could understand what I was writing), but luckily my parents recorded the tune. Three years later, I quoted it in my mini-opera, *The Sweeper of Dreams*. In 2019, I composed a few variations on this melody for the Sony Classical album. My three-year-old neighbour Antonia often came to listen and dance around when I played, so I wrote variations I hoped she would enjoy.

The Lonely Pine-Tree

I improvised this melancholy melody when I was five and called it 'The Sad Prince'. Three years later, I heard a poem by Heinrich Heine about a lonely pine-tree. I felt very sorry for the pine-tree, and adapted the "sad prince" melody to Heine's poem. The piece in this book is a transcription for piano solo:

> *Fichtenbaum und Palme* (Heinrich Heine)
>
> Ein Fichtenbaum steht einsam / Im Norden auf kahler Höh'.
> Ihn schläfert; mit weißer Decke / Umhüllen ihn Eis und Schnee.
> Er träumt von einer Palme, / Die, fern im Morgenland,
> Einsam und schweigend trauert / Auf brennender Felsenwand.
>
> There stands a lonely pine-tree / In the north, on a barren height.
> He sleeps while the ice and snowflakes / Swathe him in folds of white.
> He dreameth of a palm-tree / Far in the sunrise land,
> Lonely and silent longing / On her burning bank of sand.

Summer in Mondsee (Allegretto in A major)

When I was six, I read a fictional biography of Nannerl Mozart, Wolfgang's sister, in which she secretly composes a symphony. I immediately decided to compose a symphony myself. As I was reading, a theme in A major sprang to my mind which I thought would fit the opening of a symphony very well. Unfortunately, my parents spoiled the fun by telling me it might be more realistic to start off with a string quartet, so to humour them, I wrote it as a quartet. A few months later, I played it with three friends—the first time I played in a string quartet. The melody reminds me of the landscape of the beautiful lake Mondsee near Salzburg, where I have spent many summers. The piece in this book is a shorter piano arrangement.

Up in the Sky (Piano solo transcription of the first aria in the opera *Cinderella*)

When I was seven, I often played sonatas by Shell, a famous composer from my imaginary country, Transylvanian. There was a motif that Shell particularly liked, so I played it often, and each time developed it a bit further. When I started composing the opera Cinderella the year after, I immediately knew that this would be Cinderella's first aria. She has been up all night, forced to copy orchestral parts for the rehearsal next morning. As dawn breaks, a beautiful melody springs into her head. She tries to banish it and concentrate on copying the dreary double-bass part. But the melody won't leave her alone, and finally she gives up and bursts into song:

> Up in the sky, notes from on high, swirling around me like swallows on the wing.
> Riding the air, free as a prayer, note flies after note,
> all around they float and flutter as they sing.
> See how they rise, carefree and blithe, oh, if I could join them,
> Spreading my wings I'd soar through the air, leaving all care behind.
> Though with them I never can fly, music still can reach to the sky.
> On wings of my song I'll soar through the air, and leave all my cares behind.

When the Day Falls into Darkness (Piano transcription of Cinderella's Ballad)

This melody was actually composed by Antonin Yellowsink, my favourite composer in my imaginary land Transylvanian. When I was eight, I wrote a complete biography of Antonin, and I included in it a little sample of his compositions, with an explanation to the reader: "This beautiful expressive piece he wrote shall make you want to cry". The melody has a haunting harmony in the second bar, which I called Antonin's chord (in figured bass notation, a major F_{2-4-6} chord that appears suddenly after F minor, and resolves into minor F_{2-4-6}). I liked Antonin's harmony and melody so much that I decided to adopt it and use it in my opera. When Cinderella flees from the ball, she sings this sad melody to the prince, who is so haunted by it that he will eventually search for her throughout the kingdom, not with a shoe, but with this melody. He will sing the beginning of the tune and search for the girl who knows how to continue it:

Cinderella's Ballad

When the day falls into darkness, by the window stands a lonely child,
a flickering candle in her hand, her heart is waning like the light.
No one left to love her, no one by her side.
In the silence with no end, in the dark without a friend, she hearkens to the night.

Softly calling from the gloom she hears voices sweeter than a dream. They murmur in her ear:
"Come and join us, and together we'll be joyous, come take our hand oh you darling child.
Come and be our nearest, be our dearest, be our darling girl"
Now the voices draw so near to her and press upon her heart.

She went out into the darkness and in vain she searched both high and low,
Over field and hill and dale, wading through the blackest snow.
When the bell tolls midnight, in the dark she falls
In her ears the voices yell: "Go away you beggar girl!"
Ice has gripped her soul.

The Star of Hope (Piano transcription of duet from *Cinderella*)

Usually melodies come to me without words, but during a long car journey in Ireland, when I was nine, I was improvising in my mind, and heard a melody together with the words "even in hardship". I combined this melody with another one, which I had improvised two years earlier, in order to create the duet of the fairy and Cinderella. (I also used it in the second movement of my violin concerto, which I was writing at the same time.) Cinderella is in the depths of despair, having been left behind when everyone else has gone to the ball. She realizes that there is no one in the whole world who actually loves her. Shortly after, the fairy appears and sings Cinderella a song about a "very special star":

High over the darkness, there shines a star. Through the gloom of silence, she watches you from heaven. And if all other stars have faded, she will remain faithful and bright, and send through the night comfort and light. Even in hardship, when darkness engulfs you, look up, and you will find her. The star—her name is Hope.

In Memoriam (Adagio from Piano Concerto—melody from age ten)

A few days after my grandmother in Israel died, I was sitting at her piano in her house, and a very sad melody came to me in a sad key, B-flat minor. Although I was playing the piano, I heard in my mind the mournful tones of an oboe playing it. A year later, I used this melody in the second movement of my Piano Concerto, which starts with the oboe playing this tune. The version in this book is a shortened arrangement for piano solo, which I prepared in 2018 for a memorial service that was held at the Chancery in Vienna to commemorate the end of the Second World War.

The Chase (Impromptu in C minor)

I improvised the main melody of this piece when I was eleven. I noted it down, but didn't develop it further or use it anywhere. In June 2019, just a month before I recorded the album 'From my Book of Melodies', I decided to include this tune, so I quickly composed a short impromptu and finished it in the nick of time, just a week before the recording.

Sixty Minutes Polka

When I was twelve, a crew from the CBS television program Sixty Minutes came to my house to interview me. I improvised a little piece for Scott Pelley. In 2019, I took the two main themes from this improvisation and developed them into a bouncier piece.

I Think Of You (Piano solo transcription)

My family moved to Vienna in 2018 when I was thirteen, and as my German improved, I was excited to be able to read beautiful poems by Goethe. A melody came to me when I was reading the poem "Nearness to the beloved" (an English translation is given below), and I decided to set it to music. (Luckily I hadn't heard Schubert's setting then, otherwise I might not have had the courage to try.) I composed the song in the key of G-flat major. But a few friends who wanted to play it struggled with the many flats. So to make it easier, I've included in this book also a transposition to G major, in addition to the original key.

> *Nähe des Geliebten* (Johann Wolfgang von Goethe)
> I think of you, when the sun his beams / Over ocean flings;
> I think of you, when the moonlight gleams / In silvery springs.
> I see you, when upon the distant ridge / The dust awakes;
> In deepest night, when on the fragile bridge / The wanderer quakes.
> I hear you, when with muffled roar / the waves arise.
> I listen, when across the moor / the silence sighs.
> I am with you, as far as you may be / Yet are you near.
> The sun has set, the stars give light to me. / Would you were here!

Siren Sounds Waltz (Piano solo transcription)

As I now live in Vienna, the city of waltzes, and I love waltzing myself, I wanted to write my own waltz. A Viennese concert waltz is actually a chain of waltzes, with an introduction and a coda. In *Siren Sounds* there are four such waltzes. When I first came to Vienna, I was struck by the special sound of the Austrian police siren:

In my mind, I tried to continue this siren as a melody, and this turned into the melody of the fourth waltz in the chain. Later I included in this musical experiment siren sounds from other countries as well, especially the "wailing" police sirens. In my imagination, I tried to turn these loud and ugly sounds of the modern world into something more beautiful. In the orchestral version, the violins imitate the wailing sirens by sliding up and down the strings. Of course, the piano can't slide like the violins, so in this piano transcription you'll find scales instead. But with a bit of good will (and with plenty of pedal), one should be able to imagine the sirens nevertheless. The melody of the first waltz in the chain started out as a "happy birthday" greeting to a dear friend, David Packard.

Alma Deutscher, Autumn 2020

FOR ANTONIA

ALMA DEUTSCHER

Allegro vivace (♩ = 168)

con Ped. ad lib.

Copyright © 2019 G. Schirmer Limited
International Copyright Secured. All Rights Reserved

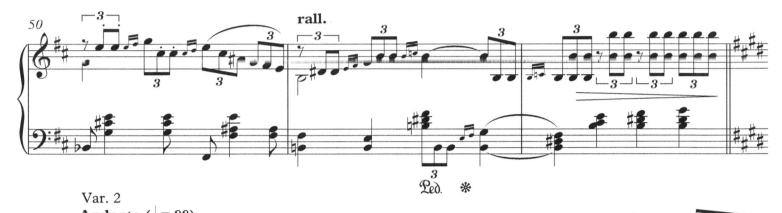

Var. 2
Andante (♩ = 88)

Var. 3
Allegretto ($\bullet$ = 124)

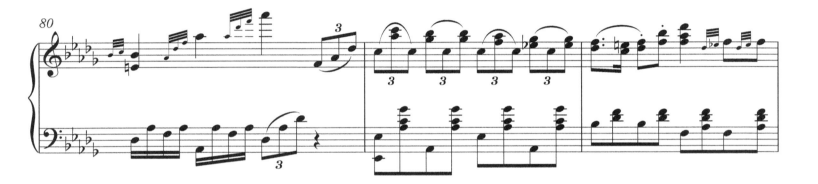

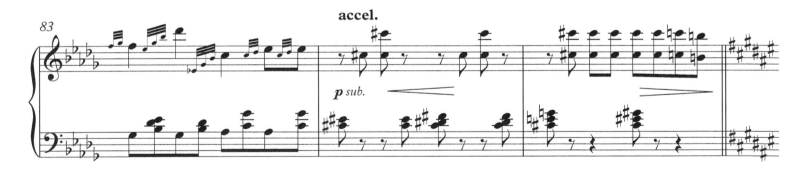

Var. 4

Più mosso (♩ = 136)

12

rall.

Var. 5
Adagio cantabile (♩ = 68)

Andante moderato (♩ = 110)

rit. _ _ _ _

Var. 6
Presto (♩ = 150)

Ped.   ✻ Ped.   ✻

THE LONELY PINE-TREE

ALMA DEUTSCHER

Copyright © 2019 G. Schirmer Limited
International Copyright Secured. All Rights Reserved

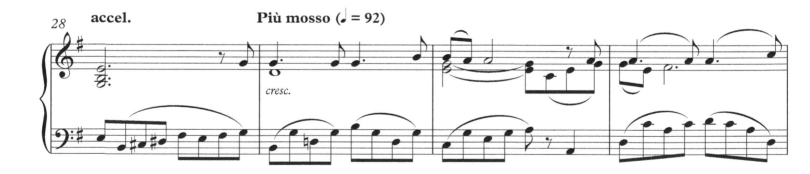

Tempo I

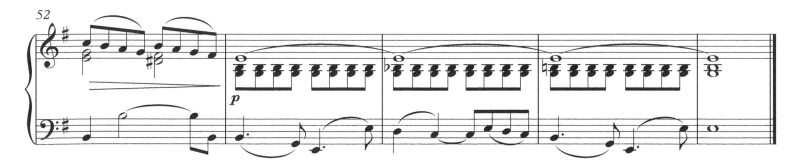

SUMMER IN MONDSEE

ALMA DEUTSCHER

Copyright © 2019 G. Schirmer Limited
International Copyright Secured. All Rights Reserved

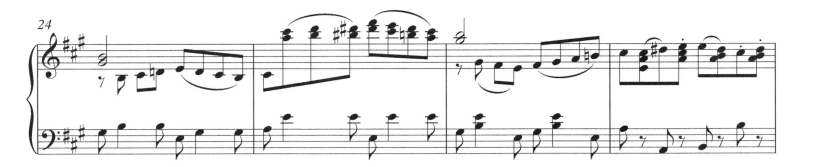

Tempo I

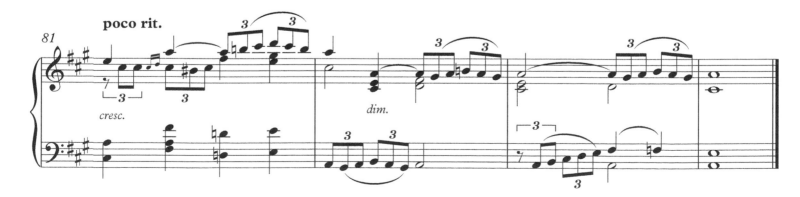

22

UP IN THE SKY

ALMA DEUTSCHER

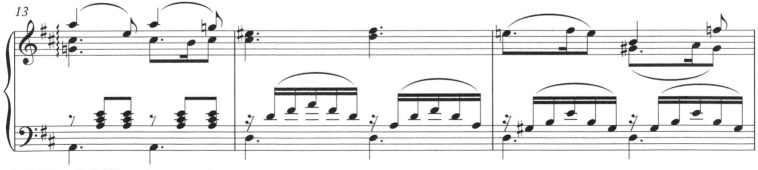

* (R.H.) and (L.H.) are just suggestions

Copyright © 2019 G. Schirmer Limited
International Copyright Secured. All Rights Reserved

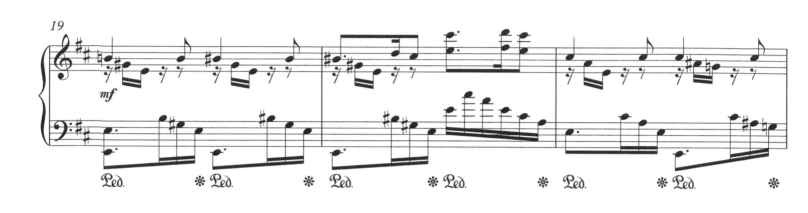

WHEN THE DAY FALLS INTO DARKNESS

ALMA DEUTSCHER

Copyright © 2019 G. Schirmer Limited
International Copyright Secured. All Rights Reserved

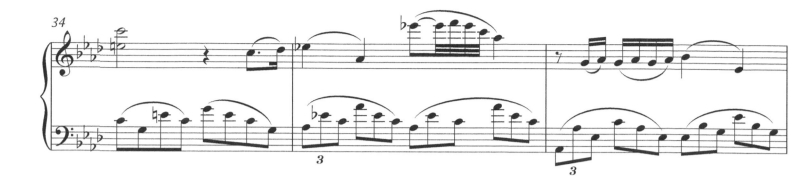

rall.   a tempo

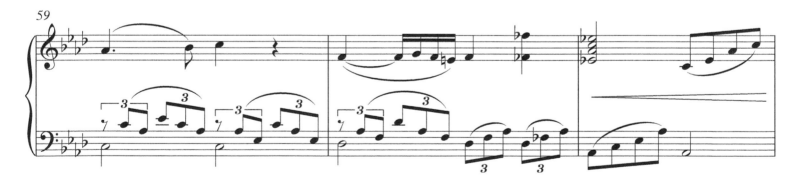

rall.   a tempo

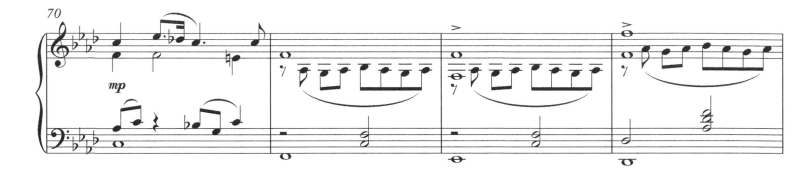

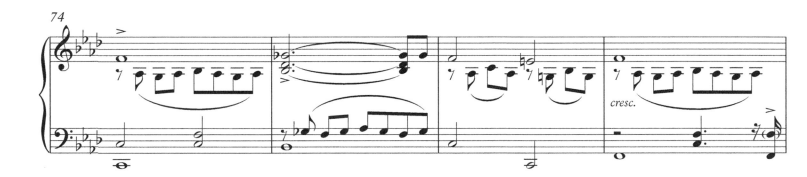

rall.

THE STAR OF HOPE

ALMA DEUTSCHER

Andante misterioso (♩ = 80)

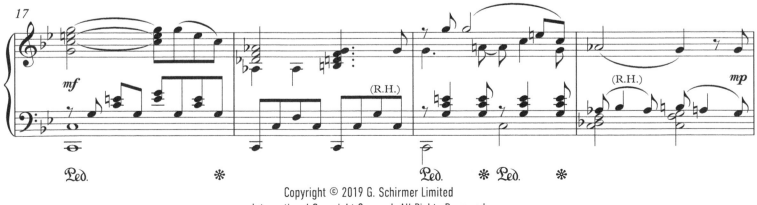

Copyright © 2019 G. Schirmer Limited
International Copyright Secured. All Rights Reserved

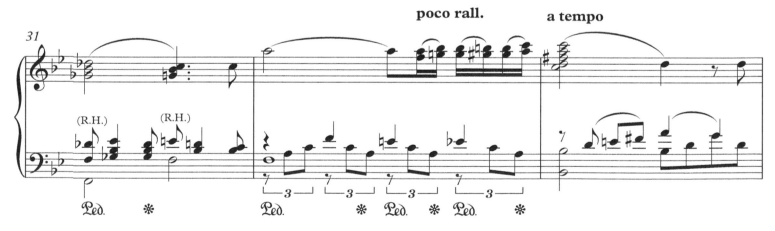

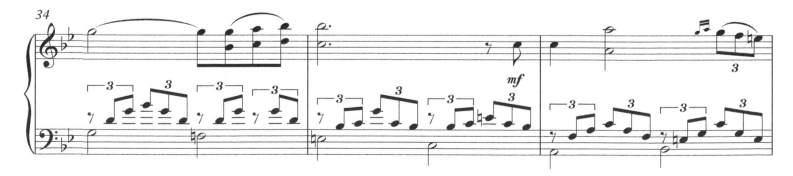

IN MEMORIAM

ALMA DEUTSCHER

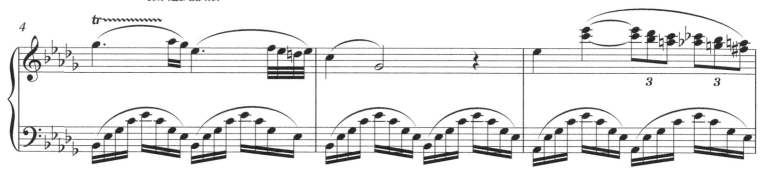

* G flat optional.

Copyright © 2019 G. Schirmer Limited
International Copyright Secured. All Rights Reserved

rit.   a tempo

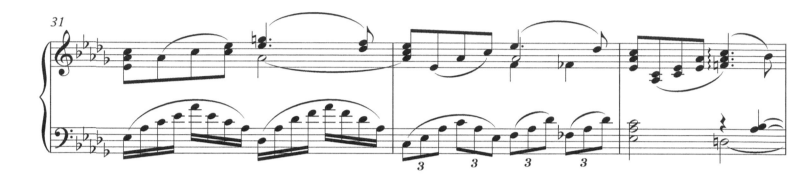

rall.   poco piu mosso

tempo primo

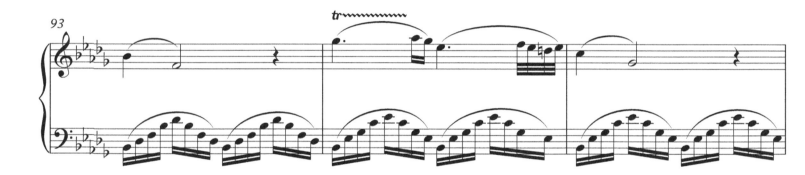

★ lower voice optional.

Ped.   ✳

40

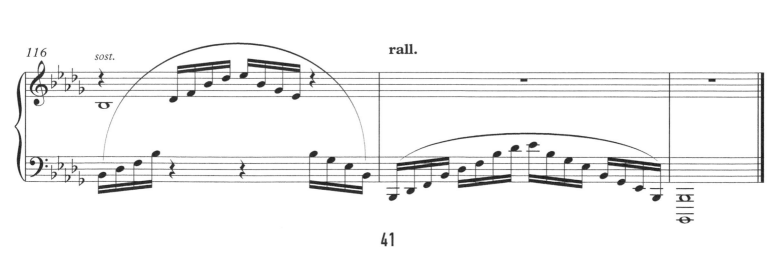

THE CHASE

ALMA DEUTSCHER

Copyright © 2019 G. Schirmer Limited
International Copyright Secured. All Rights Reserved

poco rit.   **a tempo**

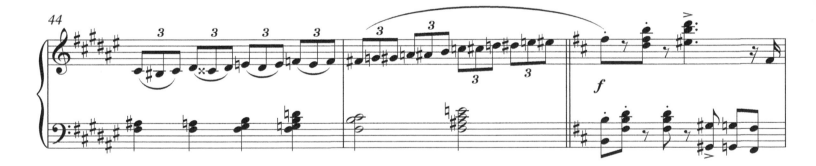

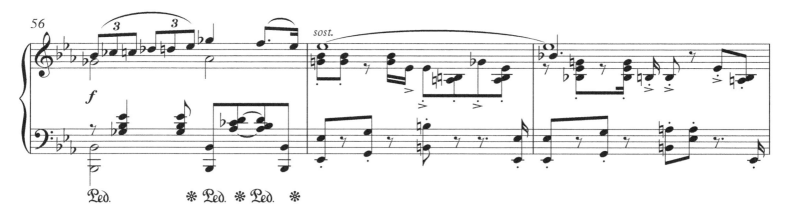

poco rit.   **a tempo**

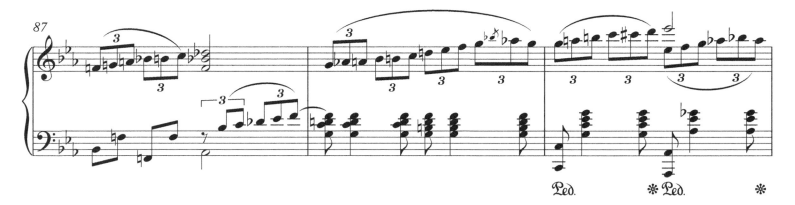

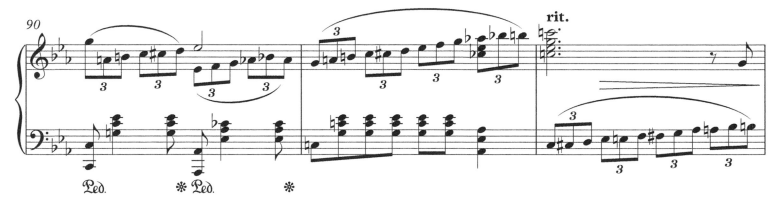

SIXTY MINUTES POLKA

ALMA DEUTSCHER

Molto vivace (♩ = 116)

Copyright © 2019 G. Schirmer Limited
International Copyright Secured. All Rights Reserved

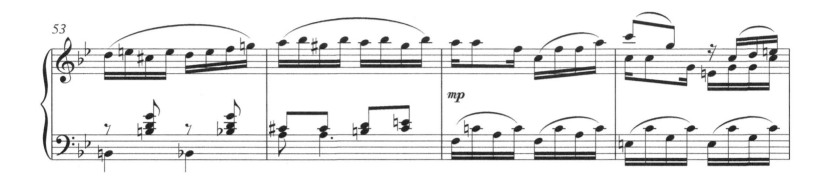

poco rit.

piu mosso

FOR DAVID AND PAM

I THINK OF YOU

ALMA DEUTSCHER

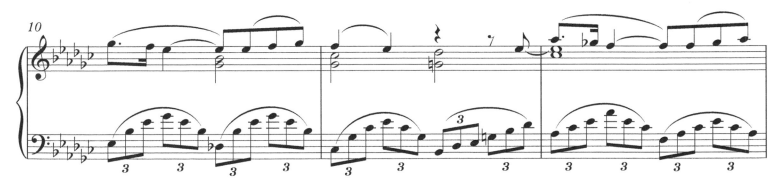

Copyright © 2019 G. Schirmer Limited
International Copyright Secured. All Rights Reserved

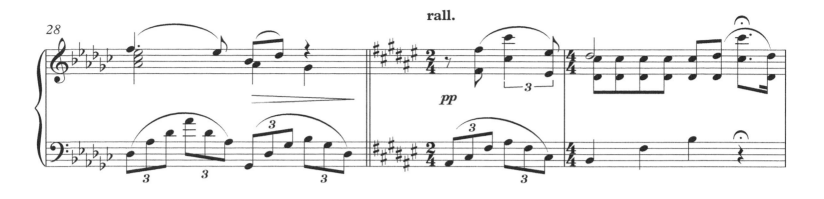

FOR DAVID AND PAM

I THINK OF YOU (G MAJOR)

ALMA DEUTSCHER

Copyright © 2019 G. Schirmer Limited
International Copyright Secured. All Rights Reserved

SIREN SOUNDS WALTZ

ALMA DEUTSCHER

*The orchestral pre-introduction, 'Street Noises', is not included in this piano version. The piece begins from the Introduction - Andante misterioso ("The ugly police sirens are gradually transformed into something beautiful.")

Copyright © 2019 G. Schirmer Limited
International Copyright Secured. All Rights Reserved

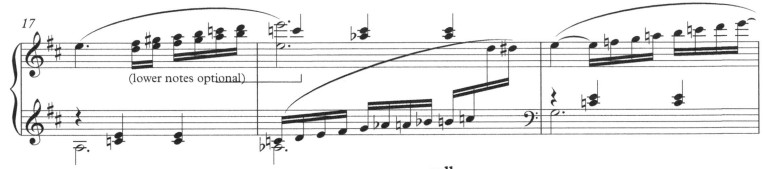

rall.

poco piu mosso

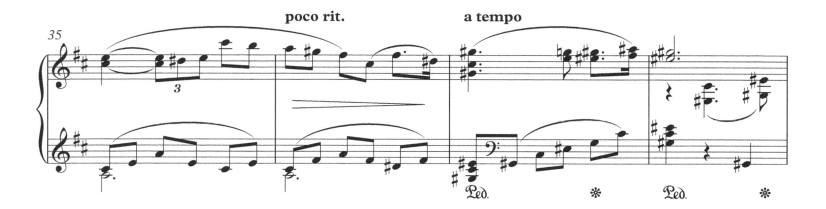

In this section dotted 8ths become:

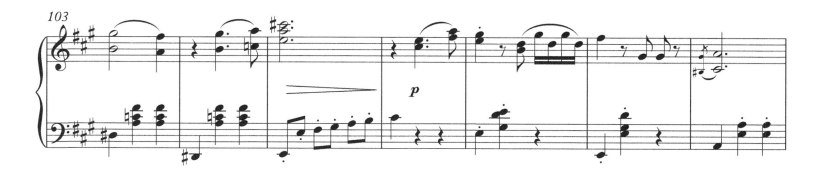

poco meno mosso

Eingang
poco accel.

174

mf

Walzer 2 (schnell)
Presto ($\quarter$ = 180)

181

188

194

poco rall.

200

68

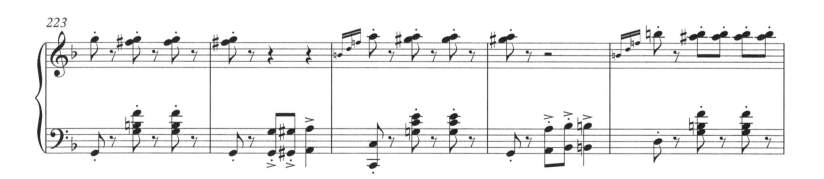

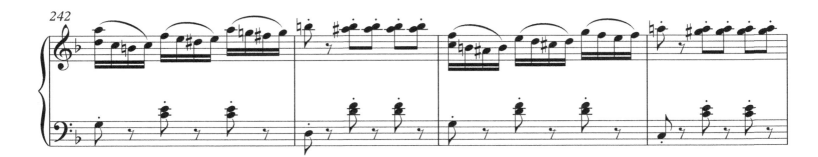

Eingang
meno mosso ma non troppo

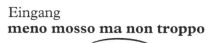

Walzer 3 (langsam)
Andante (♩ = 95)

Walzer 4 (schneller)

Allegro ($\bullet$ = 160)

poco rall.

a tempo

76

CODA*

*most of the orchestral coda is deleted in this piano version.

77

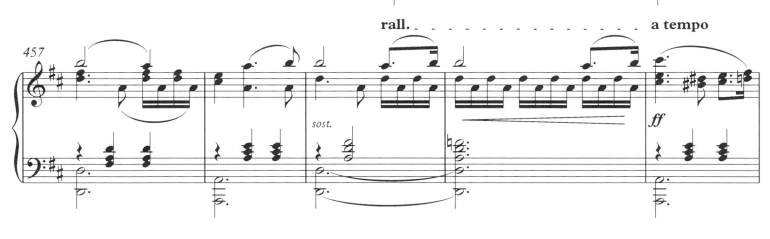

Alma Deutscher's recording *From My Book of Melodies* on Sony Classical
Available on CD & digitally
Barcode: 190759901922